OXFORD BOOKWORMS LIBRARY
*Factfiles*

# John Lennon

ALEX RAYNHAM

Stage 1 (400 headwords)

Series Editor: Rachel Bladon
Founder Factfiles Editor: Christine Lindop

# OXFORD
### UNIVERSITY PRESS

Great Clarendon Street, Oxford, OX2 6DP, United Kingdom

Oxford University Press is a department of the University of Oxford.
It furthers the University's objective of excellence in research, scholarship,
and education by publishing worldwide. Oxford is a registered trade
mark of Oxford University Press in the UK and in certain other countries

ISBN: 978 0 19 423788 8

A complete recording of this Bookworms edition of *John Lennon*
is available in an audio pack. Pack ISBN: 978 0 19 423786 4

Printed in China

Word count (main text): 5,798 words

For more information on the Oxford Bookworms Library,
visit www.oup.com/elt/gradedreaders

### ACKNOWLEDGEMENTS

*The publisher would like to thank the following for their permission to reproduce photographs:*
Alamy pp.1 (Keystone Pictures USA), 7 (Pictorial Press Ltd), 8 (Keystone Pictures USA),
15 (The Beatles/Keystone Pictures USA, Brian Epstein/Heritage Image Partnership
Ltd), 17 (record cover/Pictorial Press Ltd), 25 (Keystone Pictures USA), 30 (MARKA),
38 (newspaper/Pictorial Press Ltd), 41 (Robert Harding Picture Library Ltd), 42 (CBW),
43 (David Lyons); Corbis pp.19 (fans/Hulton-Deutsch Collection), 26 (Bettmann),
33 (march/Bettmann), 38 (fans/Bettmann), 39 (Bettmann); Getty Images pp iv
(Robert Whitaker), 2 (Michael Ochs Archives), 3, 4 (Mark and Colleen Hayward),
11 (Michael Ochs Archives), 12 (poster/GAB Archive, concert/Robert Whitaker),
13 (Michael Ochs Archives), 16 (Michael Ward), 19 (still from *A Hard Day's Night*/
Michael Ochs Archives), 20 (New York Daily News Archive), 21 (Michael Ochs
Archives), 23 (concert/Keystone, girls in sweatshirts/Keystone), 27 (Manchester Daily
Express), 29 (Express), 33 (War is Over/Three Lions), 34 (Michael Ochs Archives),
35 (Evan Agostini); Oxford University Press pp.5 (banjo), 6, 46 (MP3 screen, band, solo
guitar player, recording studio), 48 (gun, reporter, painter); Rex Features pp.9 (Sipa
Press), 17 (studio), 23 (The Beatles on a balcony/News Ltd/Newspix), 24 (Bill Zygmant),
31 (Denis Cameron), 36 (Pacific Press Service), 40 (Brian Rasic); Shutterstock
pp.5 (harmonica, piano), 10, 46 (crowd at concert, album), 48 (poster).

# CONTENTS

# 1 A man with a dream

On a warm, sunny day in June 1957, six young men stood in Rosebery Street, Liverpool, and began to play a song. The band was called The Quarrymen. They were not famous, and in 1957, they were not very good! The singer had brown eyes and brown hair, and his name was John Lennon. He sang song after song, the band played, and people danced. Nobody in the street that day knew the singer's name. But he was a man with a dream.

The Quarrymen

John Lennon, 21 years old

'One day, I'm going to be famous,' he often said. And he was right. The Quarrymen slowly became The Beatles, and seven years later, they were the world's most famous band. Before he died, John Lennon wrote and sang some of the best songs of our time.

But John Lennon was more than a singer and songwriter. He talked about love and peace, and millions of young people listened to him. He wanted to change the world. And when a man called Mark Chapman killed him, far from his Liverpool home, thousands of people stood and cried.

So how did John Lennon and his band become famous? Why did people all around the world listen to him? And why did one man want to kill him?

# 2          Liverpool boy

John Winston Lennon was born in a Liverpool hospital on 9 October 1940. Britain was at war, and John's father Alf worked on ships, so he was away most of the time. His mother Julia wanted to leave Alf, and when John was five, they asked him a question: did he want to live with his father or his mother? John did not know. He cried and went to his father at first, but when his mother walked away, he ran after her. He did not see Alf again for nineteen years.

Liverpool in the 1940s

Life was not easy for Julia, so when John was seven, he began to live with his mother's sister – his aunt Mimi – in Woolton, Liverpool. Mimi loved John, and her husband George always had time for him. George read books to John at night, and John learned to read with him. They often walked around Woolton, too. There was a big house called Strawberry Field near Mimi's house, and John liked to visit the gardens there. Years later, *Strawberry Fields Forever* became one of his most famous songs.

John visited his mother Julia a lot. She had two daughters now, but she loved John very much. Julia had lots of photos of him in the house, and she often played a record called *My Son John*. Julia listened to the radio all the time, too, so John heard the new music from the USA – rock and roll.

John with his mother, Julia

Julia sang and played the banjo and, when John was about eight, he got his first harmonica. He soon learned to play it very well. Some of John's friends had pianos at home, so he learned to play the piano, too. Then Julia taught him the banjo.

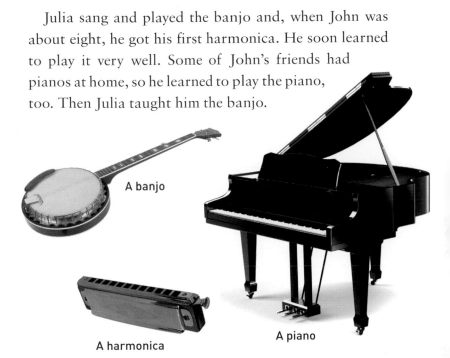

A banjo

A harmonica

A piano

Music was easy for John, and at first he was a good student at school, too. But John could not see well, and he needed glasses. Children laughed at his glasses, so he stopped wearing them. Because of this, and because he was not very interested in school work, he did not do well at high school. But at home, John did a lot of writing and beautiful art, and he read lots and lots of books.

These were happy years for John. He liked to go to the cinema with his cousins Stanley Parkes and Liela Harvey. When Stanley's family moved to Scotland, John and Liela often went there for the summer. John played his harmonica for hours and hours on the long drive to Scotland from Liverpool!

One summer, when John was away in Scotland, Mimi's husband George died. George was like a second father to John – but John never cried in front of Mimi. In 1950s Liverpool, boys did not cry.

At this time, John was becoming more and more interested in music. In 1956, a young American rock and roll singer called Elvis Presley became very famous. He was an amazing dancer, and his music was new and exciting. Elvis had seven songs in the UK music charts that year. Suddenly, young people like John wanted to sing like Elvis, dress like him, and be in a band. So Julia took John into town and bought him a guitar.

That summer, John began a skiffle band with two friends from school. They were called The Quarrymen, because their school was called Quarry Bank. Skiffle was like American country music, but faster.

Soon, there were six boys in John's band. They played songs by skiffle musicians like Lonnie Donegan. That autumn, The Quarrymen began to do little concerts, like Saturday night dances. John was the singer, and he played the guitar, too. He always played very hard on his guitar strings, so he often broke them.

It was John's last year at school, and he needed to work hard. Mimi was not happy about the band, or about his pictures and writing. Sometimes, she went into his room and took them.

'You're going to be sorry when I'm famous,' he often told her.

**A guitar**

Elvis Presley

# 3 The Beatles are born

On Saturday 6 July 1957, The Quarrymen played two concerts in Woolton, Liverpool. A fifteen-year-old boy called Paul McCartney was in the crowd that day. He was a friend of one of The Quarrymen, and he met the band and talked to John before the second concert. That day changed their lives.

When Paul met The Quarrymen between their concerts, he took one of their guitars and began playing a rock and roll song. He was amazing! John could play the first four strings of his guitar, like a four-string banjo, but Paul could play all six strings. Paul soon became one of The Quarrymen, and John quickly learned to play all six strings on the guitar.

Paul McCartney in The Quarrymen

When John left school that summer, he nearly went and worked on ships like his father. But with help from a teacher, he got into the Liverpool College of Art. Seventeen-year-old John was good at art, but he did not listen to the teachers. He often brought his guitar to college, and he dressed like a rock and roll singer.

Sometimes, John did not go to college. He met Paul in a café and they talked about books and music. You could hear great music in the cafés of Liverpool at that time. John and Paul listened to American rock and roll singers like Little Richard and Buddy Holly, and they learned to play their songs. Paul liked to write music, and in 1958, John began to write songs, too. His first song was a love song called *Hello Little Girl*.

Early in 1958, John met Paul's friend George Harrison. George was three years younger than John, but he was amazing on the guitar – so he became a Quarryman, too. The Quarrymen often met and played music in Julia's house. She was always happy when they came, and she liked to listen to their music.

George Harrison

In July 1958, something changed John's life. His mother died in a car accident. John loved his mother very much, but he never cried in front of his friends.

It was a hard time for John, but students at his art college, like Cynthia Powell and Stuart Sutcliffe, helped him a lot. Cynthia was John's girlfriend, and Stuart Sutcliffe was his best friend. One day, Stuart bought a bass guitar. He played that bass guitar for hours every day because he wanted to be in John's band, but he was not very good. Stuart was an artist, not a musician.

Many different people played with The Quarrymen, but slowly the band became John, Paul, and George on guitars, and later, Stuart on the bass guitar. Paul, George, and Stuart were not from Quarry Bank High School, so the band changed their name. The Quarrymen became The Beatals, then The Silver Beetles.

They played in cafés and music clubs like the Casbah Coffee Club, but they did not get a lot of money for their concerts. There were lots of young bands in Liverpool – and The Silver Beetles were not the best!

**A bass guitar**

John and Stuart often went to a café called the Jacaranda Club. The café manager, Allan Williams, knew a lot of bands, and in 1960, he found work for them in Scotland with a singer called Johnny Gentle. The band were very excited about their first tour, but it was not easy. They ate and stayed in some very bad places because they did not have any money. In the end, Stuart's mother bought train tickets home for them.

Later, Williams found work for them in Hamburg, Germany – for more money. For the first time, they had a drummer. His name was Pete Best. They had a new name, too: The Beatles.

**Pete Best with The Beatles**

Williams drove them to Germany, and when they stopped in the Netherlands, John took a harmonica from a music shop and did not pay for it. Many years later, John Lennon fans went to the Netherlands, found the shop, and paid for that harmonica.

From August to November 1960, The Beatles played at two different night clubs in Hamburg. They stayed in some very bad rooms, and they played for five, six, or seven hours every

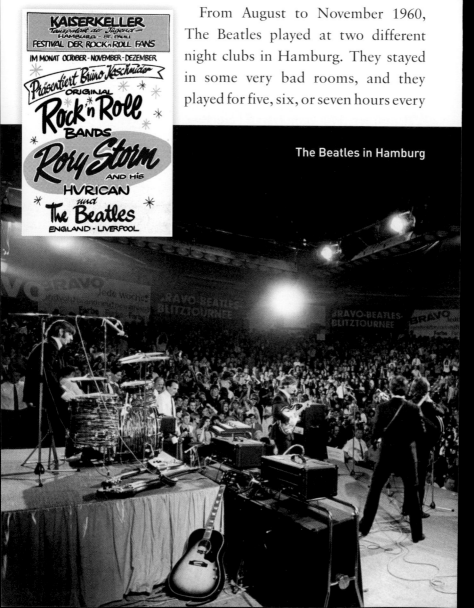

The Beatles in Hamburg

night of the week. At one of the clubs, they performed with a Liverpool band, and they became friends with the drummer – Ringo Starr. The bands finished work at 3 a.m., and then they all went out for breakfast!

The clubs were in the worst streets of Hamburg. Every night, people threw bottles and chairs – and sometimes knives – across the room. It was very, very hard for The Beatles, but they did not stop playing.

'One day we're going to be famous,' they thought.

Ringo Starr

# 4 Beatlemania

In December 1960, The Beatles were back in England. There were only four of them now, because Stuart Sutcliffe stayed in Hamburg. Nobody in Liverpool remembered the band. But when they began to play at a concert there one night, everyone became very excited. They moved nearer to the front, and some people began to scream!

The Beatles' music was different now, after Hamburg. It was not skiffle or rock and roll – it was something new and exciting, and people loved it. Everyone began to talk about The Beatles. In April 1961, John, Paul, George, and Pete played most nights in clubs all around Liverpool – and the clubs sold every ticket!

That spring, The Beatles went back to Hamburg for four months, and they recorded songs there with a singer called Tony Sheridan. Then, in November, they played in a Liverpool club called the Cavern Club. It was not a big club, and it was hot, dark, smoky, and noisy. But some of the best bands in Liverpool – and in Britain – played there.

A young man called Brian Epstein saw The Beatles at the Cavern Club. Epstein did not often listen to bands, and he was not a band manager before he met John, Paul, George, and Pete – he had a record shop. But he knew a lot about music, and he loved The Beatles. He came back and watched the band many times in the next few weeks. The Beatles liked him, and he soon became their manager.

Epstein quickly changed The Beatles' hair and clothes. They wore suits now, so they looked different from most bands, and people remembered them. Epstein looked for a record company for The Beatles, too. Bands become famous because record companies make and sell their records, so this was important for The Beatles. But for a long time, no record companies were interested.

Then, someone from Decca Records saw the band and liked them, so The Beatles performed for the record company on New Year's Day, 1962. But they did not play well that day, and Decca did not want to make their records.

Brian Epstein

At the Cavern Club

In August 1962, Ringo Starr became The Beatles' new drummer, and Pete Best left the band. John married his girlfriend Cynthia Powell that month, too. But he did not see his new wife very much: The Beatles had concerts every night!

That summer, they began to play at the Cavern Club all the time. Slowly, more people became interested in Liverpool music. TV and magazine reporters from Europe and the USA visited the club, and they began to talk about Liverpool music, or 'Liverpop'.

After a lot of work, Brian Epstein now had a record company for The Beatles. Parlophone (EMI) began to record their songs. In October 1962, The Beatles' first record, the song *Love Me Do*, was number 17 in the British music charts. It was an exciting time for the band.

In February 1963, The Beatles had their first number one hit with a John Lennon song, *Please Please Me*. Later, there was an album called *Please Please Me*, too, and The Beatles recorded all fourteen songs in one day! John Lennon was ill that day, and the band played for ten hours, but he sang amazingly.

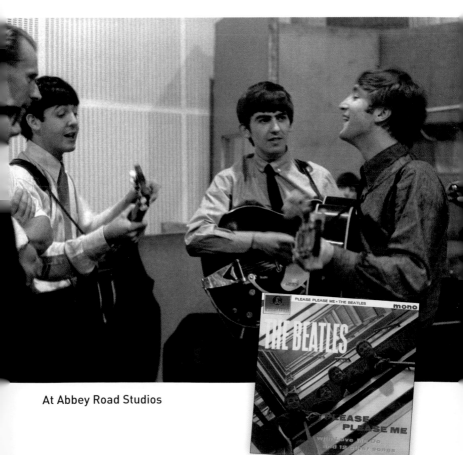

**At Abbey Road Studios**

Three more of The Beatles' songs were number one in 1963. The band became famous because of their records, and it happened very fast. In October, they came to London and were on TV. Fifteen million people watched them on TV, and thousands of fans waited outside the TV studio. People screamed and stopped cars in the street. One reporter called it 'Beatlemania'.

People cried and screamed at every Beatles concert. Fans waited outside their hotels, too – sometimes all night in the cold and rain. In The Beatles' first film, *A Hard Day's Night*, John, Paul, George, and Ringo run away from their fans. In Britain, that was their life.

People loved The Beatles because their songs were great, and you could easily remember and sing them. The Beatles were young like their fans, and they looked good, too. But The Beatles became famous because they worked very hard. They played or recorded seven days a week, and John and Paul wrote new songs at night in their hotel rooms. Between 1960 and 1964, The Beatles performed for about 1,200 hours – most bands do not play that much in their lives!

In November 1964, The Beatles did a big concert in Liverpool. Thousands of fans were in the streets, and more people stood in windows and on roofs.

'We want The Beatles!' people cried, and the noise was amazing. These four young men from Liverpool were now Britain's most famous faces.

*A Hard Day's Night*

Beatlemania in London

# 5  World-famous

In the autumn of 1963, a famous American magazine laughed at British Beatles fans for their crying and screaming. But soon, Beatlemania arrived in the USA. In February 1964, The Beatles' song *I Want to Hold Your Hand* was number one in the American charts. That month, when The Beatles went to the USA, five thousand fans waited for their plane at New York's John F. Kennedy airport.

**Arriving in New York**

On 9 February, 73 million people watched The Beatles on the famous *Ed Sullivan Show* on American TV. In the New York studio, people screamed when The Beatles began to play. Outside, thousands of fans stood on Broadway and 53rd Street. No one could get through the streets.

American stars like Elvis Presley were famous in Britain. Now, suddenly, Americans loved a British band. Later, British bands and singers like the Rolling Stones and Elton John became famous in the USA, too – but it all began with The Beatles, that night in New York City.

The Beatles played two concerts on their first visit to the USA – in Washington, D.C. and New York City. But they came back again in August 1964 for a one-month, thirty-concert tour of Canada and the USA. On 23 August 1964, The Beatles performed at the Hollywood Bowl in Los Angeles. After the concert, they met some of Hollywood's rich and famous. When John was a boy, he watched these film stars in the Woolton cinema with his cousins. Now they wanted to meet him!

In the next two years, The Beatles went on tours to many countries, and there was Beatlemania around the world. People nearly died in crowds in the Philippines. In New Zealand, hundreds of fans stopped The Beatles' car, and they could not get out. In Tokyo, the band could not leave their hotel because there were thousands of fans outside. So John, Paul, George, and Ringo sat in their hotel room and made a picture. Years later, somebody bought it for $155,000!

On their third American tour in 1965, The Beatles visited Elvis at his house in Los Angeles. They sat and talked about music, then they began to play guitar with him. It was amazing for John, because Elvis was his hero. Friends watched while the two greatest names in music – The Beatles and Elvis – played together!

When The Beatles were not on tour, they recorded music in London. Between 1963 and 1965, they made six albums, and lots of their songs, like *Can't Buy Me Love*,

A *Ticket to Ride*, and *We Can Work it Out*, were number one in Britain and the USA. Thousands of people bought the records, and fans could buy Beatles T-shirts, guitars, magazines, and lots more things, too.

New York, 1964

Melbourne, 1964

Tokyo, 1966

The Beatles became very rich, and John Lennon bought a big house and a very expensive car. The money was great, but some things were not easy. The Beatles could not go out for dinner or go to the shops because fans ran after them, and they quickly became tired of this. And they were not happy with their concerts because people screamed, and nobody could hear their music. Some of John and Paul's songs at this time, like *Help*, were not happy ones.

John Lennon's Rolls Royce

Because people loved The Beatles, they watched them on TV and read about them in magazines all the time. But sometimes The Beatles did not think carefully before they spoke. In July 1966, John said something to a magazine reporter, and American fans became very angry when they read about it. On The Beatles' fourth tour of the USA, people broke Beatles records in the street and protested outside the concerts.

Some people wrote angry letters, too. 'You're going to die,' some of them said, and Brian Epstein was afraid. 'Is somebody going to shoot John Lennon?' he thought.

# 6         Family man

In April 1964, a man walked into Brian Epstein's office and said, 'I'm John Lennon's father.' When John saw Alf Lennon, he was not happy. He thought, 'Do I want to meet my father again after nineteen years? Why did he go away all those years ago? Why did he not visit or write?' John could not forget these things. He met his father sometimes after that, but they never became good friends.

John's family life was not easy. He and Cynthia had a son now, called Julian. John wanted to be a good father to Julian, but he did not have much time with his family.

With Cynthia and Julian

The Beatles were always on tour, or at the recording studios in London, so Cynthia and Julian often did not see John for weeks. And when he was at home, he worked very hard. He wrote songs all the time, and he wrote two books, too.

In the winter of 1966, John met a Japanese artist called Yoko Ono in London. They soon became very good friends. Yoko was seven years older than John, but she was very like him. She was an artist and musician, too, and like John, Yoko had a young child – a daughter called Kyoko.

John and Cynthia soon broke up, and after that he was with Yoko all the time. They made art together, and Yoko came to the studio when The Beatles recorded their music.

With Yoko Ono

**With Yoko Ono and Julian**

On 20 March 1969, Yoko and John got married in Gibraltar. Yoko Ono became Yoko Ono Lennon, and John later changed his name to John Ono Lennon. That summer, they bought a beautiful house called Tittenhurst Park. Everything in the rooms was white, and they had a beautiful garden and a recording studio. Yoko and John were happy there, and they recorded some amazing songs in the studio.

Julian often came to the house, and he played with Kyoko. John and Yoko loved to do things with the children. One year, they all went on holiday to Scotland, because John remembered happy summers there with his cousins.

# 7                                  Going solo

On 29 August 1966, The Beatles performed at Candlestick Park, San Francisco. Twenty-five thousand fans listened to The Beatles that cold summer evening, but it was the band's last big concert. The Beatles did not need to do concerts and tours now. They could work in a studio, and sell millions of records. They were afraid of the crowds at concerts, too – some fans got too excited.

A year after the San Francisco concert, Brian Epstein died. He was only thirty-two years old. Epstein was an amazing manager, and a great friend, too. It was very hard for The Beatles because they were musicians, not managers. They did not manage the band well after Epstein died. They began a company called Apple, but the company lost a lot of money, and things were not easy between John, Paul, George, and Ringo.

On a cold winter's day in January 1969, The Beatles played together for the last time. They performed for a film on a roof in London. People stood in the street and listened. Office workers looked out of windows. Taxi drivers stopped their cars. They could not see the people on the roof, but everybody knew their songs. In the end, the police came onto the roof and stopped them, because of the noise!

A year later, the band began to break up. Many of their fans could not understand it. But The Beatles all

London, January 1969

wanted to do different things now, and they wanted to write different music. In 1970, all four Beatles made solo albums. After that, the four of them never played together again.

John Lennon made eight solo albums – most of them in the USA. When John wrote songs for The Beatles, they were usually about love. But the songs on his solo albums were often about the world around him, or about his life. Some of them are very sad. His second album, called *Imagine*, became one of the most important albums of all time.

In New York City

1971 was an important year for John and Yoko: they moved to the USA. They found a house in Greenwich Village, in Manhattan, and they were very happy there.

New York in the 1970s was the most exciting city in the world. John and Yoko's door was always open, and they met lots of interesting people. They knew many of the best artists, writers, and musicians of their time. John and Yoko went around the city on bicycles, and John loved his life there.

# 8 War and peace

The day after John and Yoko got married in 1969, they went to Amsterdam. It was an interesting week for a new husband and wife. For seven days, they sat on their hotel bed and talked to reporters about peace. They called their war protest a 'bed-in', and it was on TV around the world.

At the time, there were wars in many countries, like Northern Ireland, Nigeria, and Mozambique. One of the worst wars was in Vietnam: half a million Americans went and fought there, and every day, hundreds of people died. Many people wanted to stop the war.

The Amsterdam bed-in protest

The second bed-in protest was in Montreal, Canada in May 1969. One day, John recorded a song called *Give Peace a Chance*. There were many people in their room that day – reporters, musicians, and friends. John played the guitar and sang, and everyone became the band. They hit the tables with their hands and sang with him. It became the most famous song of the Vietnam War protest. On 15 November that year, hundreds of thousands of people sang *Give Peace a Chance* outside the White House in Washington, D.C.

Later that year, John recorded a song called *Happy Christmas (War is Over)*, and John and Yoko paid for posters in ten cities around the world. The posters said 'WAR IS OVER (if you want it)' in many different languages. This was John and Yoko's message to the world.

After John and Yoko moved to the USA, John talked about peace on TV, and he went to many protests about wars and spoke to the crowds. Millions of young Americans listened to him, and the government was not happy. The FBI (government police) began to watch John, and they listened to his telephone.

In 1972, the government wrote him a letter. You must leave the country, the letter said. Yoko and John wanted to stay in the USA, so they talked to a lawyer called Leon Wildes. Wildes was not very interested in John's war protests or his music, but he worked very hard for John and Yoko. It took four years, but in the end, John Lennon could live freely in the USA.

John liked the work of Gandhi and Martin Luther King. These men changed the world, but they did not do

Peace protest, Manhattan

John and Yoko's poster in New York City

it with guns – they changed it with love, protests, and peace. Before John Lennon, rock stars and film stars did not usually talk about peace, or changing the world. Today, people like Bono, Angelina Jolie, and George Clooney work hard for peace, and they help thousands of people around the world.

# 9               A quiet life

9 October 1975 was a very important day for John and Yoko. Their son Sean Taro Lennon was born – on John's thirty-fifth birthday. When John's first son Julian was born, he did not see him very much because he was in The Beatles. This time, he wanted to be a better father, so he stopped making music.

John became a 'house husband'. Yoko worked, and John stayed at home all day with Sean. They often went out for lunch or dinner, or shopping, and they played with their cats. John did everything for Sean, and he sang to him at night. Julian sometimes visited them in the USA, too. Mimi never came to New York, but John often asked her. She was afraid of the USA because many Americans had guns.

With Sean

The Dakota

John and Yoko now lived in a famous New York building called The Dakota. From their windows, you could see the trees and gardens of Central Park. John and Yoko took Sean to Central Park all the time. New Yorkers often saw them when they walked there. 'Hey, John. How are you?' people called. But fans did not run after him. John loved that.

John did not make any albums for five years, but he bought records and listened to the latest music – from glam rock to punk. He worked on his third book, too, and wrote lots of letters – to friends, family, and fans. He did some art, and he made nice dinners at home. And he learned some Japanese, because John, Yoko, and Sean went to Japan in 1977. They stayed there all summer, and John and Sean met Yoko's family for the first time.

The Lennons usually lived in their home in The Dakota, but they had a beautiful house near the sea on Long Island, too. John learned to sail there, and he loved it.

In June 1980, John sailed from Rhode Island to Bermuda with some friends. At first, everything went well. But then some very bad Atlantic weather hit them. Some of John's friends became ill, so for hours, John did all the sailing. He was afraid, but he stood out there in the rain and sang songs.

Sean and Yoko met John and his friends when they arrived in Hamilton, Bermuda, and John stayed there with Sean for two months. He began to work on a new album, and he wrote some great songs, like *Woman* and *Beautiful Boy*. Then, one day, he saw a beautiful flower in the gardens in Hamilton. It was called 'Double Fantasy', and John loved the name. When he went back to New York, John wanted to record an album called *Double Fantasy*.

John was excited about music again, and he began to record new songs. One day that autumn, John and Yoko were in the recording studio all night. In the morning, they heard John's first new record, the song *(Just Like) Starting Over*, on the radio. They were very happy, and they danced around the room!

In the studio with Yoko Ono

# 10          Dead heroes

On 9 October 1980, Sean and John had their fifth and fortieth birthdays. Fans waited outside The Dakota, and at 5 p.m., they looked up and saw planes in the sky. The planes wrote a message: 'Happy Birthday John and Sean – love Yoko.'

Eight thousand kilometres away in Hawaii, it was eleven o'clock in the morning, and a man called Mark David Chapman could hear something in his head: 'Kill someone famous!' Two weeks after John's birthday, Chapman bought a gun, got a plane to New York City and visited The Dakota. But he could not buy bullets for his gun in New York City, so he left.

On 5 December, John talked to a reporter from a music magazine about the film star James Dean. James Dean died very young, and he became a hero for young people.

'I don't want to be a dead hero,' John said.

The next day, Mark Chapman came back to New York City. This time, he had bullets.

On Monday 8 December 1980, John and Yoko left The Dakota at around 5 p.m. Chapman came up to them. He had John's new *Double Fantasy* album, and John wrote on it for him. John and Yoko worked in the recording studio that evening, and John phoned Mimi. At about 10.45 p.m., John and Yoko came back home. Their driver often drove the car into The Dakota, but it was a nice evening, so this time he stopped outside in the street. John and Yoko got out of the car.

Chapman was in the street near the door of The Dakota. He took out his gun and shot John Lennon four times. Then he sat and waited for the police.

An ambulance arrived very quickly, and took John to Roosevelt Hospital, but he was dead when he arrived there. Soon, TV across the USA and the world told people: 'John Lennon is dead.'

Crowds of people came to The Dakota.

'He's not dead! It's not true!' one girl cried. But it was.

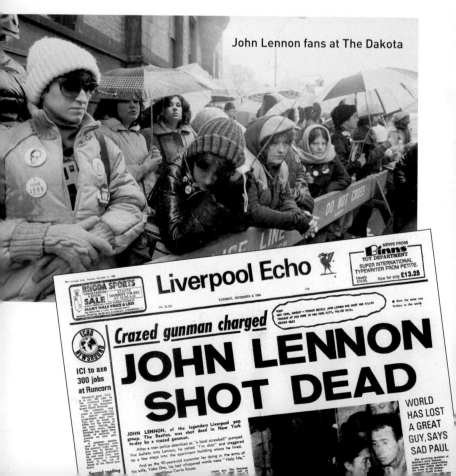

John Lennon fans at The Dakota

The next Sunday in Liverpool, thousands of people stood in the streets. They remembered their city's dead hero, and they listened to his songs. Across the Atlantic in New York City's Central Park, a crowd of 150,000 people stood in the cold. Some quietly cried. Some sang John Lennon's songs. They had photos of John and big messages.

'Why?' read one message.

'We'll never forget you,' read another.

Crowds in Central Park, 14 December 1980

And they did not. New York City was John's second home, and now there is a place in Central Park called Strawberry Fields, like John's famous song. It is a quiet place, and people sit there and think. There is a memorial at Strawberry Fields, too – a circle with the word 'Imagine' in it. People leave flowers on the circle, and sometimes people leave their guitars.

Every year on 8 December, people meet in Central Park. They remember John's life, and they sing his songs. Thousands came in 2010, thirty years after he died.

# 11 Remembering John Lennon

There are many John Lennon statues and John Lennon memorials around the world. One of the best statues is near the old Cavern Club in Liverpool. It is John when he was a young Beatle. He is standing next to a building with his hands in his pockets – a young man with a big dream.

The year after John died, George Harrison wrote a song about his old friend, and George, Paul, and Ringo recorded it. Later, Paul McCartney remembered John in his song *Here Today*. There were songs by bands and singers like the Cranberries, Queen, and Elton John, too.

Paul, George, and Ringo all became solo musicians after The Beatles broke up, and they all performed at concerts around the world. Paul McCartney became one of the greatest British singers of his time. George Harrison died in 2001, but Paul and Ringo never stopped performing.

John Lennon statue, Liverpool

Julian and Sean Lennon became musicians like their father. They want to make the world a better place, and they do a lot of important work and help many different people.

Yoko Ono finished John Lennon's last album after he died, and his last book, too. She became an important artist, musician, and peace worker. She never left The Dakota: she stayed there because she wanted to remember all the good times there with him.

After John died, many fans wanted to buy some of his things, like letters, or albums with his writing on them. In 1982, someone bought his car for $2.23 million! But most people want to remember the man and his music. There are lots of books, magazines, and films about John Lennon, and two hundred thousand people buy his albums every year.

When many people think about John Lennon, they remember his song *Imagine*. It became one of the most important songs of all time, but it was John Lennon's message to the world, too.

*Imagine* is a song about living together – in a world without hungry people and war. In the video for *Imagine*, John is sitting at a white piano in a white room, but the shutters on the windows are closed. Then Yoko opens the shutters, the summer sun comes into the room, and John sings. He sings of his dream, and it is a beautiful one: a dream of a better world for everyone.

# GLOSSARY

**amazing** *(adj)*  when something is exciting and interesting
**around** *(prep)*  in different places; on all sides of something
**art** *(n)*  beautiful things, like pictures
**artist** *(n)*  An artist makes music or art.
**become** *(v)*  to begin to be something (past tense **became**)
**birthday** *(n)*  the day you were born
**break up** *(v)*  to stop being together (past tense **broke up**)
**bullet** *(n)*  A person puts a bullet in a gun before they shoot it.
**buy** *(v)*  to give money because you want something (past tense **bought**)
**café** *(n)*  You can get drinks and food in a café.
**chart** *(n)*  the best-selling songs of the week
**city** *(n)*  a big and important town
**club** *(n)*  People can listen to music, dance, etc. in a club.
**college** *(n)*  You go to a college to learn after you leave school.
**company** *(n)*  In a company, people make or sell things.
**cousin** *(n)*  the child of your mother or father's brother or sister
**crowd** *(n)*  a lot of people
**dance** *(v)*  to move your body to music
**dream** *(n)*  when you want to have or be something
**drummer** *(n)*  A drummer plays the drums, a musical instrument; you hit the drums with your hands or with sticks.
**fan** *(n)*  A fan likes somebody or something very much.
**fight** *(v)*  to push and hit someone (past tense **fought**)
**film** *(n)*  a story in moving pictures on television or at the cinema
**glasses** *(n)*  Some people can see better when they wear glasses.
**government** *(n)*  the people who control a country
**great** *(adj)*  very, very good
**gun** *(n)*  A gun shoots out bullets and kills people or animals.
**hard** *(adj)*  not easy; *(adv)* a lot
**hero** *(n)*  A hero does something good or very hard.
**lawyer** *(n)*  A lawyer knows about law: rules for what people can or cannot do in a country.

**life** *(n)*  a person's time of being alive

**magazine** *(n)*  a small book with lots of pictures in it

**manager** *(n)*  the most important person in a company or shop

**marry** *(v)*  to become somebody's husband or wife

**memorial** *(n)*  a thing, place, or building made for remembering someone or something

**message** *(n)*  words from one person to another person

**outside** *(prep)*  not in a building

**park** *(n)*  a place with no buildings, often in a town or city

**pay** *(v)*  to give somebody money for something (past tense **paid**)

**peace** *(n)*  a time with no war

**perform** *(v)*  to play music in front of other people

**place** *(n)*  where something or somebody is

**police** *(n)*  The police stop people when they break laws.

**protest** *(v & n)*  to talk angrily or do things because you do not like something

**reporter** *(n)*  When things happen, a reporter writes or talks about them in newspapers or on the radio or television.

**roof** *(n)*  the top of a building or car; it goes over your head

**sail** *(v)*  to go on water in a ship or boat

**scream** *(v)*  to make a big noise because you are afraid or hurt

**sell** *(v)*  to give something to somebody for money (past tense **sold**)

**shoot** *(v)*  to hurt or kill with a gun (past tense **shot**)

**shutter** *(n)*  a thing for a window, usually made of metal or wood; when you close it, the room becomes dark

**solo** *(adj)*  without other people

**star** *(n)*  a famous person, like a singer

**throw** *(v)*  to move something through the air from one place to another with your arm (past tense **threw**)

**together** *(adv)*  with someone or with people

**tour** *(n)*  a visit to lots of different places

**T-shirt** *(n)*  clothes for the top part of your body, when it is warm

**war** *(n)*  fighting between countries or between people

**world** *(n)*  the Earth with all its countries and people

# SOME MUSIC WORDS

**music** *(n)*  You make music when you sing or play instruments.

**album** *(n)*  a group of songs by one musician or band

**band** *(n)*  The people in a band play music together.

**concert** *(n)*  when a person or a band plays music to lots of people in a club or a theatre

**musician** *(n)*  A musician sings or writes music, or plays a musical instrument.

**record** *(n)*  You can listen to music on a record; *(v)* to put music onto a record, CD, etc.

**recording studio** *(n)*  People make records in a recording studio.

ACTIVITIES

*Before reading*

1 Match the words below to the pictures.

*artist __ / gun __ / poster __ / reporter __*

1       2       3       4

2 How much do you know about John Lennon? Choose the correct words to complete the sentences.

1 John Lennon was born in *1900 / 1940*.
2 He was a singer and a *writer / sports person*.
3 He lived and worked in Britain and *France / America*.
4 He married *one time / two times*.
5 He was in a band called The *Beatles / Rolling Stones*.

3 Match the names below to the sentences.

*Elvis Presley / Mark Chapman / Paul McCartney / Yoko Ono*

This person...
1 was in The Beatles with John Lennon.
2 was an artist, and John Lennon's wife.
3 was a famous American singer.
4 killed John Lennon.

ACTIVITIES

## *While reading*

**Read Chapter 1. Match the two parts of the sentences.**

1 John Lennon was the...
2 In 1957, John Lennon's band were...
3 John Lennon wanted...
4 Later, the band became...
5 John Lennon wrote...
6 John Lennon wanted to...

a not very good.
b change the world.
c world famous.
d to be famous.
e some amazing songs.
f singer of The Quarrymen.

**Read Chapter 2. Match the names below to the sentences.**

*Alf Lennon / Elvis Presley / George / Julia Lennon / Mimi /
Stanley Parkes*

1 John did not see this person for nineteen years.
2 This person taught John to play the banjo.
3 John often stayed with this person in Scotland.
4 John lived with this aunt.
5 This person was like a father to John.
6 John wanted to be like this person.

**Read Chapter 3. Put the events in order.**

a The band become the Silver Beetles.

b The band go on their first tour.

c John meets Paul McCartney at a Quarrymen concert.

d Julia dies in a car accident.

e The Beatles go to Hamburg.

f John leaves school.

**Read Chapter 4. Are these sentences true or false? Change one word to correct the false sentences.**

1 Everyone in Liverpool remembered The Beatles when they came back from Hamburg.

2 The Beatles recorded songs with Tony Sheridan.

3 Brian Epstein had a clothes shop.

4 Ringo Starr became The Beatles' new drummer.

5 *A Hard Day's Night* was The Beatles' first song.

6 The Beatles worked five days a week.

**Read Chapter 5. Choose the correct words to complete the sentences.**

1 The Beatles were the *first / last* really famous British band in America.

2 They met Elvis Presley at *the Hollywood Bowl / his home in Los Angeles.*

3 The Beatles could not leave their hotel in Tokyo because of the *weather / fans.*

4 They could not *hear / buy* their music at concerts.

5 On their last American tour, people *sang / protested* outside The Beatles' concerts.

**Read Chapter 6. Are the sentences true, false, or not mentioned in the chapter?**

1  John's father was very happy when he met his son again.
2  John saw his son Julian every day.
3   John and Yoko Ono were together a lot in the late 1960s.
4  Yoko and John were not very happy at Tittenhurst Park.

**Read Chapter 7. Correct the <u>underlined</u> words to make true sentences.**

1  The Beatles <u>found</u> a lot of money when they began Apple.
2  They played on a roof in London, but the <u>fans</u> stopped their concert.
3  John Lennon's <u>first</u> solo album became very important.
4  New <u>Delhi</u> in the 1970s was the world's most exciting city.
5  John Lennon made eight <u>Beatles</u> albums.

**Read Chapter 8. Complete the paragraph with six of the words below.**

*bed / government / lawyer / leave / married / protest /
reporters / stay / Vietnam / wars / Washington*

The day after John and Yoko got [1]_____, they flew to Amsterdam and began a peace [2]_____. They sat on a hotel [3]_____ for seven days and talked to [4]_____ about peace. At the time, there were a lot of [5]_____ around the world, in places like [6]_____. John and Yoko wanted people to stop fighting.

**Read Chapter 9. Complete the sentences with the names of people or places.**

1 _____ was born on John's 35th birthday.
2 _____ never came to New York City.
3 John and Yoko's home in New York City was a famous building called _____.
4 The Lennons also had a home by the sea on

_____.

5 In 1980, John Lennon and some friends sailed to

_____.

**Read Chapter 10. Put the events of 8 December 1980 in order.**

a John's car stopped outside The Dakota at 10.45 p.m.
b An ambulance took John to hospital, but he died.
c Chapman stayed and waited for the police.
d Crowds of people came to The Dakota.
e John wrote something for Chapman.
f Chapman took out his gun and shot John Lennon.
g John and Yoko worked at the recording studio.

**Read Chapter 11. Are the sentences true, false, or not mentioned in the chapter?**

1 Paul, George, and Ringo did not record any more songs after John died.
2 Paul and Ringo often meet.
3 Yoko Ono still lives in New York.
4 John Lennon's sons are not like their father.
5 Nobody listens to John Lennon's music today.
6 John Lennon thought that *Imagine* was his best song.

## ACTIVITIES

### *After reading*

## Vocabulary

**1 Find the words in the wordsearch.**

| | | | | | | | |
|---|---|---|---|---|---|---|---|
| S | S | O | L | O | T | R | D |
| M | A | N | A | G | E | R | R |
| C | I | A | L | W | U | B | E |
| R | L | K | B | M | W | N | A |
| O | E | R | U | R | A | R | M |
| W | Y | A | M | F | R | F | I |
| D | E | P | E | A | C | E | L |
| C | O | N | C | E | R | T | D |
| M | E | M | O | R | I | A | L |

1 When there is no fighting. (*n*)
2 This person looks after a band. (*n*)
3 When you want to have or be something. (*v* / *n*)
4 A record with lots of songs. (*n*)
5 This person loves your music. (*n*)
6 A place to remember someone. (*n*)
7 When countries fight. (*n*)
8 To travel in a boat. (*v*)
9 One person did this album. (*adj*)
10 A lot of people in one place. (*n*)
11 When bands play to their fans. (*n*)
12 You hit this to make music. (*n*)
13 This place in a city has trees. (*n*)

## Grammar

1  **Write sentences in the past simple. Use the correct form of the verbs.**

1  John / meet / Paul McCartney in 1957.

2  Decca Records / not want / to record The Beatles' songs.

3  the band / become / famous the next year.

4  Yoko and John / move / to America.

5  they / protest / about wars.

6  Mark Chapman / shoot / John in New York.

2  **Choose the correct words to complete the text.**

¹*Nobody / Nothing* knew The Beatles when they came back from Hamburg, but ²*someone / everything* changed one night in December 1960. ³*Everyone / Nobody* became very excited at a Beatles concert, and soon ⁴*no one / everybody* in Liverpool began to talk about them. ⁵*Everything / Everyone* happened very fast after that – ⁶*nobody / someone* at Parlophone liked their music, and they began to make records. ⁷*Everyone / Someone* loved their songs, and ⁸*something / everything* went well for The Beatles after that. For a long time, ⁹*nothing / somebody* could stop them!

# Reading

**1  Match the song titles with their descriptions.**

*A Hard Day's Night / Beautiful Boy / Give Peace a Chance / Hello Little Girl / Imagine / I Want to Hold Your Hand / Love Me Do / Strawberry Fields Forever*

This was...

1  John Lennon's first song.
2  a song about a place near Aunt Mimi's house.
3  The Beatles' first record.
4  a Beatles film.
5  number one in the USA in February 1964.
6  John's second solo album.
7  an important protest song.
8  a song for Sean Lennon.

**2  Put the events of John Lennon's life in the correct order.**

a  John's second child is born.
b  John meets Yoko Ono in London.
c  Brian Epstein becomes The Beatles' manager.
d  The Beatles play their first concerts in Hamburg.
e  The Beatles break up.
f  People sing John's songs in Central Park.
g  John meets Paul McCartney.
h  John starts The Quarrymen.

## Writing

1 Read the news report. Then answer the questions.

# The new stars of Liverpool

Go to the Cavern Club any night, and you can hear The Beatles – one of Britain's best young bands. Their music is fast, exciting, and great to dance to – and fans scream and cry at their concerts!

The band began in Liverpool and then worked in Hamburg. Now they're back in Liverpool – and everyone is talking about them! Soon all of Britain is going to know the names John, Paul, George, and Ringo.

1 Did the writer write this *before / after* the band's first number one?
2 Is the writer talking about the band's *albums / concerts*?

2 Now write a news report about The Beatles' first visit to America. Use the information in chapter 5 to help you.

3 Choose one of the headlines and write a short news report.

IT ISN'T EASY TO BE A BEATLE

JOHN AND YOKO MARRY IN GIBRALTAR

JOHN LENNON IS SHOT DEAD

# Speaking

**1  Do you agree or disagree with these statements?**

1  Julia sang and played the banjo, so it was easy for John to learn music.

2  I think The Beatles became famous because they worked really hard.

3  John could do anything. For example, he was also an artist and a writer.

4  I don't think The Beatles were as good as today's bands.

5  John wrote his best songs after he left The Beatles. For instance, *Imagine* and *Beautiful Boy* are amazing.

6  In my opinion, John wasn't happy before he met Yoko.

**2  Underline the words and phrases in exercise 1 that:**

- give opinions
- give examples
- say what happens because of something

**3 You are going to make a film about John Lennon's life. Discuss these questions in pairs. Use the words and phrases in exercises 1 and 2.**

1  Who are the most important people in the film?

2  Which film stars are going to play these people?

3  When does your film start? (For example, when John is born; when he's at art college; when he's a Beatle.)

# INDEX

# THE OXFORD BOOKWORMS LIBRARY

**THE OXFORD BOOKWORMS LIBRARY** is a best-selling series of graded readers which provides authentic and enjoyable reading in English. It includes a wide range of original and adapted texts: classic and modern fiction, non-fiction, and plays. There are more than 250 Bookworms to choose from, in seven carefully graded language stages that go from beginner to advanced level.

---

Each Bookworms Factfile has full colour photographs, and offers extensive support, including:

- ▸ extra support pages, including a glossary of above-level words
- ▸ activities to develop language and communication skills
- ▸ a complete audio recording
- ▸ online tests

Each Bookworm pack contains a reader and audio.

| | | |
|---|---|---|
| **4** | **STAGE 4** ▸ 1400 HEADWORDS | ▸ CEFR B1–B2 |
| **3** | **STAGE 3** ▸ 1000 HEADWORDS | ▸ CEFR B1 |
| **2** | **STAGE 2** ▸ 700 HEADWORDS | ▸ CEFR A2–B1 |
| **1** | **STAGE 1** ▸ 400 HEADWORDS | ▸ CEFR A1–A2 |

Find a full list of *Bookworms* and resources at
**www.oup.com/elt/gradedreaders**

If you liked this stage 1 Factfile,
why not try...

### New York
JOHN ESCOTT

New York is big, noisy, and exciting, and it is waiting for you. Open the book and come with us to this wonderful city.